This book belongs to

_____

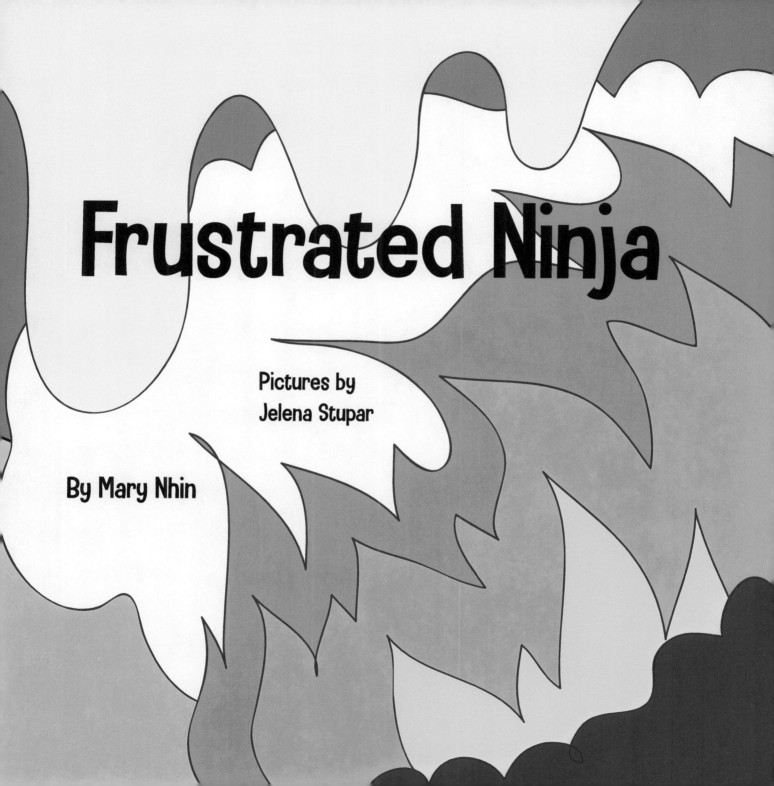

Frustrated Ninja

Pictures by
Jelena Stupar

By Mary Nhin

Even though I followed the directions, my slime was too runny. I could have gotten frustrated, but instead I stayed calm and spoke positively to myself.

I've learned to recognize that hot feeling of frustration and put the flames out.

For example, when I don't understand how to do something,
I ask for help.

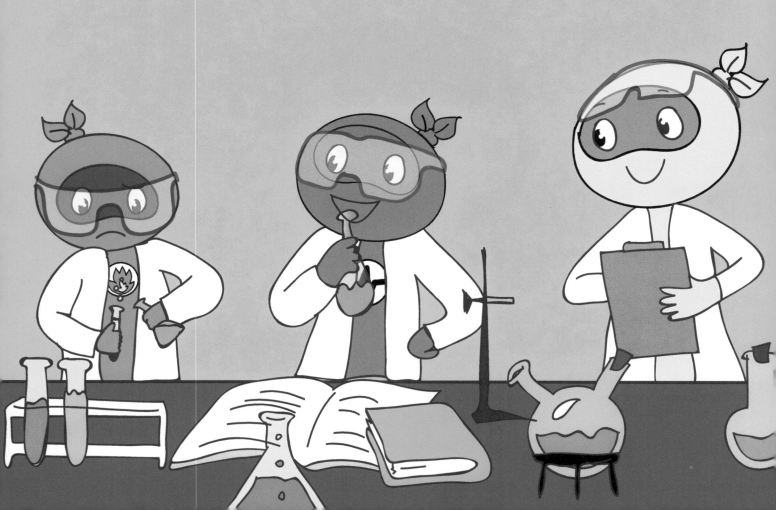

During school, when I ask to do something and my teacher tells me no, I calmly tell myself...

When I lose or make a mistake, I take a deep breath and count to ten.

I used to not know what to do when I got frustrated. I would just react.

Each time I got frustrated, I could feel my muscles tighten up. I would start to feel hot inside, and sometimes I would have trouble thinking.

Then, I would start to feel out of control.

In the past, when I was asked to put away my electronics,
I got so frustrated, I would say unkind words.

If I made a mistake, I threw myself on the floor, kicked my feet, and screamed.

And whenever someone didn't want to play or hang out with me, I would push or throw things.

But things changed one day when I lost a game. I got so frustrated, throwing my controller across the room. It barely missed Impulsive Ninja.

I felt bad I acted that way and went to find my friend.

I'm sorry. I don't know why I did that.

It's okay to feel frustrated. It's normal. But acting that way when we are upset won't solve any problems, and we might hurt ourselves or another person.

Hit people
Push or throw things
Say unkind words
Throw yourself on the floor and kick your feet
Scream

But there is something we can do about our frustration. When we start to feel frustrated, remember to be like a firefighter and calm down the frustration flames before they turn into a big fire.

To calm down the frustration flames, we can use some of the tools firefighters use to put out frustration flames:

Write down our worries and problems in a journal.
Go outside for a walk to tap into our five senses.
Listen to music, color, or journal.
Count to 10.
STOP and take a deep breath.
Squeeze a pillow, toy, or play dough.

The next day I tried to be aware of the feelings I had including any frustration. Several times throughout the day, I recognized that hot feeling of frustration and immediately pretended I was a firefighter putting out the hot flames.

I was able to better manage my frustration from then on.

I continue to pretend I'm a firefighter by calming down the frustration flames when I get hot.

Frustrated Ninja's Poem

When I get hot, it's my body's communication
That what I'm feeling is frustration.
I choose to STOP and put the fire out.
Because calm is what I'm all about.

Fight hot feelings of frustration by calming down the flames before they become a big fire!

Please download your Frustrated Ninja Activity Bundle Kit and check out our beyond the book resources at ninjalifehacks.tv

@marynhin   @GrowGrit
#NinjaLifeHacks

Mary Nhin   Ninja Life Hacks

Ninja Life Hacks

CPSIA information can be obtained
at www.ICGtesting.com
Printed in the USA
BVHW011527190723
667495BV00006B/36